Nonprofit Quick Guide™

Building a Five-star Board

Linda Lysakowski, ACFRE
Joanne Oppelt, MHA

Nonprofit Quick Guide: Building a Five-star Board

One of the **Nonprofit Quick Guide**™ series

Published by Joanne Oppelt Consulting, LLC

Copyright © 2020 by Linda Lysakowski and Joanne Oppelt

ISBN Print Book: 978-1-951978-04-4

13 12 11 10 9 8 7 6 5 4 3 2 1

Printed in the United States of America

About the Authors

LINDA LYSAKOWSKI, ACFRE

Linda is one of approximately one hundred professionals worldwide to hold the Advanced Certified Fundraising Executive designation. Linda is the author of ten nonfiction books, a contributing author, coeditor, or coauthor of at least seventeen others. She has also written six books in the fiction realm.

Linda has more than thirty years in the development field. She worked for a university and a museum before starting her own consulting firm. In her twenty-seven years as a philanthropic consultant, Linda has managed capital campaigns that have raised more than $50 million, helped hundreds of nonprofit organizations achieve their development goals, and trained more than forty thousand development professionals in most of the fifty states of the United States, Canada, Mexico, Egypt, and Bermuda.

She served on the Association of Fundraising Philanthropy (AFP) Foundation for Philanthropy Board and on the Professional Advancement Division for AFP. She is a past president of the Eastern Pennsylvania and Sierra (Nevada) AFP chapters. She received the Outstanding Fundraiser of the Year award from the Eastern Pennsylvania, Las Vegas, and Sierra (Nevada) chapters of AFP, was honored with the Barbara Marion Award for Outstanding Service to AFP, and received the Lifetime Achievement Award from the Las Vegas AFP chapter.

Linda is a graduate of Alvernia University with majors in banking and finance as well as theology/philosophy, and a minor in communications. As a graduate of AFP's Faculty Training Academy, she is a Master Teacher.

JOANNE OPPELT, MHA

Joanne, principal of Joanne Oppelt Consulting, LLC, is a seasoned rainmaker with a distinguished track record of success. During her thirty-plus years working in the nonprofit arena, she built or rebuilt successful fundraising departments at every stop, helping her organizations grow capacity and more effectively fulfill their missions.

She has held positions from grantwriter to executive director at the nonprofits Community Access Unlimited, Caring Contact: A Listening Community, Family to Family Network of New Jersey, Christian Healthcare Center, March of Dimes Central New Jersey, Prevent Child Abuse New Jersey, and Maternal and Family Health Services. Her extensive background in a variety of work roles and organizations enables her to understand the realities and challenges nonprofit practitioners face—both internally and externally. Her track record of success positions her to help any nonprofit, whether through her books, training, coaching, or consulting practice, turn around struggling fundraising operations.

Joanne is the author of four books and coauthor of twelve. She has taught at Kean University as an Adjunct Professor in its graduate program. She is also a highly sought-after speaker and presenter.

Joanne holds a master's degree in health administration from Wilkes University, where she graduated with distinction. Her bachelor's degree is in education, with a minor in psychology.

Dedication

Dedicated to the thousands of nonprofit board members engaged in the noble work of changing lives and saving lives.

Contents

Chapter One

What is a Five-star Board Member?

We all want to have five-star board members, right? So, what makes a good board member? It comes down to five simple criteria:

- ◆ Board members believe in the mission of the organizations for which they serve.
- ◆ They understand the difference between governance and management.
- ◆ They know their roles and responsibilities.
- ◆ They are willing to support the organization with their time, talent, and treasure.
- ◆ They are eager to support the organization's fundraising efforts.

Belief in the Mission

Belief in the organization's mission is the most vital part of serving on the board of a nonprofit. Board members must be enthused about the mission of the nonprofit to be a strong supporter of it. Jerold Panas described this as being a "roaring advocate" for the organization. We think he hit the nail on the head. One Vice President of Institutional Advancement at a small university said she only asked three things of her board members—that they have the university "in their minds, in their hearts, and on their lips." You can't ask for a better commitment from board members. If you have these "roaring advocates," you will have a five-star board.

Governance versus Management

Board members need to understand the difference between governance and management clearly. We like to explain this difference simply. Governance: think of the governor of your state—it is not the role of the governor to fill potholes on the roads in your state. It is, however, the governor's role to assure that the Department of Transportation is managing the highways and byways of your state to ensure safety for residents and anyone driving through.

Similarly, it is not the role of the board to decide what color stationery you use, how much personal time off is given to staff, or whether you have filtered water in the staff break room. It is, however, the board's role to make sure the organization is adequately staffed and that the executive director is capable of hiring the right people to make the day-to-day decisions that affect the organization.

Roles and Responsibilities

There are essential roles boards play in a nonprofit organization. There are roles of the board as a whole and responsibilities of individual board members. It is vital that you have these roles and responsibilities written down and that they are shared with existing and prospective board members. In the next chapter, we'll go into more detail about assessing how individual board members meet these responsibilities. But here are some roles the board, as a whole, fills:

Determine the Organization's Mission and Purpose

A statement of mission and purpose should articulate the organization's goals, means, and primary constituents served. It is the board's responsibility to create the mission statement and review it periodically for accuracy and validity. Each board member should fully understand and support it. (Goals and purpose can be revised as needed, but the mission does typically not change.)

Select the Chief Executive Officer

Boards must reach a consensus on the executive director's job description and undertake a careful search process to find the most qualified individual for the position. The Chief Executive Officer is the only staff member who reports to the board. The rest of the staff report to the executive director.

Support the Executive and Review Executive's Performance

The board should ensure that the executive director has the moral and professional support needed to further the goals of the organization. The executive director, in partnership with the entire board, should decide upon a periodic evaluation of the executive director's performance.

Ensure Effective Organizational Planning

As stewards of an organization, boards must actively participate with the staff in an overall strategic planning process and assist in implementing the plan's goals.

Ensure Adequate Resources

One of the board's foremost responsibilities is to provide adequate resources for the organization to fulfill its mission. The board should work in partnership with the executive director and staff to raise funds from the community.

Manage Resources Effectively

The board, to remain accountable to its donors and the public and to safeguard its tax-exempt status, must assist in developing the annual budget and ensure that proper financial controls are in place.

Determine and Monitor the Organization's Programs and Services

The board's role in this area is to determine which programs are the most consistent with an organization's mission and to monitor their effectiveness.

Enhance the Organization's Public Image

An organization's primary link to the community—including constituents, the public, and the media—is the board. The board's role in clearly articulating the organization's mission, accomplishments, and goals to the public, as well as garnering support from prominent members of the community, is an essential element of a comprehensive public relations strategy developed by the staff.

Assess Its Own Performance

By evaluating its performance in fulfilling its responsibilities, the board can recognize its achievements and reach a consensus on which areas need to be improved. Discussing the results of a self-assessment at a retreat can assist in developing a long-range plan.

Time, Talent, and Treasure—The Role of the Board in Fundraising

One way to build capacity for your organization is by strengthening the fundraising ability of your board. Okay, we know what you're thinking: "We can't get our board to help with fundraising; they aren't the 'movers and shakers' in town." If this is a statement you have heard in your organization, read on!

While some organizations do not set fundraising as a priority for their board members, most nonprofits benefit from having a board more actively using their connections to help the organization.

The key to getting your board to embrace fundraising lies in three simple steps: the recruitment process, assuring that board members are committed to the organization, and removing the fear of fundraising that is inherent in most people.

Once you have a board that understands its role in fundraising and consists of members who have a real passion for your mission, it will be easy to get them motivated to embrace this role.

Take the fear out of fundraising by providing ongoing training and education about fundraising for the board. Remember the old saying, "No money, no mission." It's not about raising money for the organization's coffers. It's about fulfilling the mission of the organization. When board members are passionate about the mission, they will understand that you need the money to support this mission. You can provide a fifteen-minute segment at each board meeting on some aspect of fundraising or periodic all-day training sessions on essential elements of your fundraising program. You can also invite board members to attend educational programs run by the Association of Fundraising Professionals (AFP), or a myriad of webinars that are available on fundraising.

Teaming up board members with another board member, a staff member, or a volunteer more experienced in fundraising will help put the reluctant board member at ease.

Once your board members understand the art and science of fundraising, they'll be more inclined to get involved.

Wrapping It Up

◆ Good board members are "roaring advocates" for your organization.

◆ Boards must first understand the difference between governance and management.

◆ Spell out the roles and responsibilities of the board.

◆ If you recruit and train board members in the right way, they will be not only willing but eager to give and get money for the organization. We'll be discussing board recruitment more in the following chapters.

Chapter Two

How Do Your Board Members Measure Up?

How many stars would you give your board right now? You may have some five-star members and some one-star members. The five-star board members will attend meetings and events regularly, serve on committees, act as ambassadors, and enthusiastically support the organization. The one-star members are the ones you don't see at board meetings, don't support the organization financially or otherwise, and may even be contentious in their relations with other board members, staff, or clients. So, let's analyze your board.

What Should Your Board Members Be Doing?

What are the responsibilities of an individual board member? Not only does the board as a whole have roles and responsibilities, but individual board members need to be held accountable for fulfilling obligations, such as:

◆ Attending board and committee meetings and functions, such as special events;

◆ Being informed about the organization's mission, services, policies, and programs;

◆ Reviewing the agenda and supporting materials before board and committee meetings;

◆ Serving on committees and offer to take on special assignments;

◆ Making a meaningful personal financial contribution to the organization;

◆ Informing others about the organization;

◆ Suggesting possible nominees to the board who can make significant contributions to the work of the board and the organization;

◆ Keeping up to date on developments in the organization's field;

◆ Following conflict-of-interest and confidentiality policies;

◆ Refraining from making special requests of the staff; and

◆ Assisting the board in carrying out its fiduciary responsibilities, such as reviewing the organization's annual financial statements.

Following are some personal characteristics to consider when seeking new board members or analyzing current board members:

◆ Are they able to listen, analyze, think clearly and creatively, and work well with people individually and in a group?

◆ Are they willing to prepare for and attend board and committee meetings, ask questions, take responsibility, and follow through on a given assignment, generously contribute personal and financial resources, open doors in the community, and evaluate themselves? Even if your board doesn't think they have the right connections, with the proper education, they will come to realize that they do know people who can be supportive of your organization in many ways.

◆ Are they willing to develop skills they do not already possess, such as to cultivate and solicit funds, cultivate and recruit board members and other volunteers, read and understand financial statements, and learn more about the substantive program area of the organization? While this might seem like rocket science to some board members, they don't have to be financial geniuses or program experts. Training sessions held by staff or outside experts can easily transmit the information board members need to be effective.

◆ Do they possess honesty; sensitivity to and tolerance of differing views; a friendly, responsive, and patient approach; community-building skills; personal integrity; a developed sense of values; concern for your nonprofit's development; and a sense of humor?

What Should Your Board Structure Look Like?

While every board is different, typically boards function best when they are large enough to have an active committee structure, with a different chair for each committee. Most committees should also include non-board members to allow you to draw on a broader array of expertise. Plus, this is a great "training ground" for potential new board members. Here is just one sample of what a larger board structure could look like.

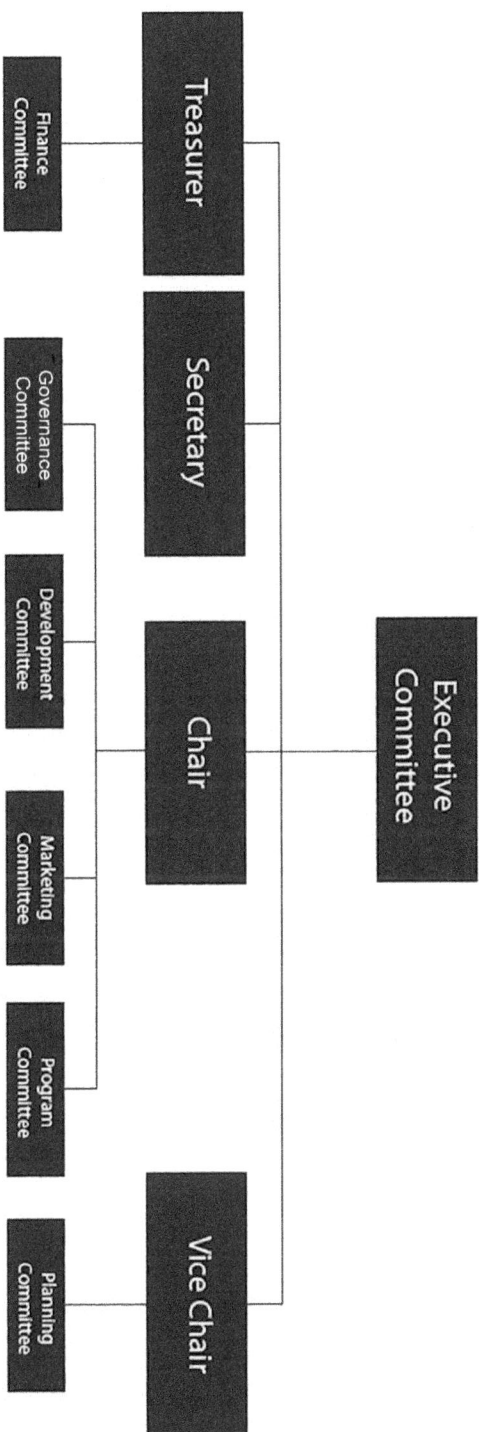

Assessing Your Board

There are numerous tools available to help you assess your board. In fact, in Linda's course, ***Build a Great Board*** (visit Linda's website at https://lindalysakowskicourses.com if interested), she provides many tools to help you assess existing board members and potential board members, as well as evaluating your board as a whole. Some things you should assess on at least an annual basis:

◆ The demographic makeup of your board members (age, gender, ethnic, and geographic diversity);

◆ The skills and talents of your board members;

◆ The board contributions of time, talent, and treasure;

◆ Attendance and participation at board meetings;

◆ The board's willingness to act as ambassadors for your organization; and

◆ The board's involvement in fundraising.

Once you've evaluated your board and each board member using the tools available through Linda's course or through tools you find through other means, you need to make some tough decisions. Are there board members you need to "fire"? Can you help improve results with some training and education? What should you be looking for when replacing board members? If you need help with this, you can contact a governance consultant or the authors of this book.

Restructuring Your Board

When all else fails, you may need to look seriously at your board and restructure it with people who are willing and able to be involved in fundraising. Following are some ways to help you restructure your board:

◆ Make sure to include a provision in your board position description that outlines the board member's expected involvement in meetings, events, and your fundraising program.

◆ Be sure that the governance committee reviews this provision with all prospective new board members and that the potential board members agree to it *before* being invited to serve on the board.

◆ Make sure to enforce term limits.

◆ If some of your board members refuse to participate in activities, events, and fundraising, do not nominate them for another term when their first term on the board expires.

◆ Ask your board chair or the chair of your development committee to speak privately to board members who are not participating in board functions and encourage them to get involved.

◆ Plan educational sessions on various aspects of program, governance, and fundraising so board members will understand fundraising strategies and feel more comfortable with the process.

Wrapping It Up

◆ You need a job description that clearly outlines board responsibilities so you can evaluate how closely board members are following expectations.

◆ The board should be evaluating itself and its performance annually.

◆ Individual board members should be evaluated annually on their performance.

◆ Self-evaluation is important.

◆ Committees should be active and pertinent to your origination's needs.

◆ Most committees will benefit from having non-board members on them.

◆ Term limits are essential.

◆ Once the evaluation process is complete, you need to decide whether training and education are needed, whether you need to "fire" some board members, and what you should be looking for in new board members.

Chapter Three

Building a Board That Engages in Fundraising

First, remember that your board members are your chief advocates and hold legal and fiduciary responsibility to ensure that resources are obtained for and allocated to mission fulfillment. As the leaders of the nonprofit, they set the example for others.

Board members must contribute at a significant level for them if they expect others to give significantly as well. Plus, it is essential to remember that if board members don't give, they will not be good at fundraising. So, let's start with some basic principles for board giving:

◆ Board members are (or should be) selected because they believe in the mission of your organization, so they should also have the desire to support the agency financially.

◆ It will be challenging to ask the public to support your special events if your board members do not attend these events.

◆ Members of your community will generally contribute more to your organization when they are asked by a volunteer whom they know than if a paid staff member asks them.

◆ Ultimately, board members have assumed the responsibility for implementing the mission of your agency, and raising funds is a critical component of this responsibility.

◆ Many foundations and other donors will not contribute if they do not see 100 percent board participation.

If your board members are reluctant to assume their fundraising role, you might start by getting them involved in some "painless" ways of fundraising:

◆ Help plan fundraising activities.

◆ Develop and review mailing lists and potential major donor lists.

◆ Sell tickets for an event (without the pressure of "every board member needs to sell fifty tickets").

◆ Serve on an event committee.

◆ Ask friends and family to contribute to your organization instead of birthday, anniversary, or other special-occasion gifts.

◆ Ask companies they do business with to sponsor an event, take out an ad in a program book for an event, or make an outright donation.

◆ Sign appeal letters to individuals they know.

◆ Participate in a "thankathon" in which they call current donors just to thank them for their gifts, not to ask for money.

◆ Attend a donor recruitment event.

◆ Plan a donor thank-you event.

Getting Your Board Enthused about Fundraising

◆ Help board members understand their role in fundraising by including it in their job description and by holding an educational session led by an outside "expert."

◆ Assess your organization's fundraising activities, and make sure board members aren't "nickeled and dimed" at every board meeting.

◆ Stress the importance of having a development plan that spells out the fundraising roles of the board, staff, and volunteers.

◆ Establish a development committee that includes both board and non-board members.

◆ Select a board member who "gets it" about fundraising and have this individual chair your development committee.

◆ Provide fundraising training for board members in specific areas they feel they need help understanding, i.e., planned giving, capital campaigns, social media, or telephone fundraising.

◆ If you are the chief development officer, ask the board chair and CEO to allow your input to the board recruitment process so that the board will include more people who are willing to be involved in your fundraising program.

Board Giving

A few months ago, Linda taught several webinars about board giving. Out of the more than one-hundred people joining the webinar, just two of the people on the webinar had 100 percent giving from their boards. They attended the class because they wanted to learn more about board giving. Linda polled the groups several times and found a few interesting things:

◆ The average board size was twenty-one, with a low of three for a start-up organization to a high of fifty, proving that the size of the board didn't affect its percentage of giving.

◆ The average rate of board giving was at 56 percent, with a low of zero percent and a high of 100 percent.

◆ Most people said their board doesn't get involved in fundraising because they don't know how, think it's not their job, or simply have a "tin-cup mentality."

◆ Many solicit their board members at recruitment, at orientation, or at board meetings. Several are doing it right—as part of their annual appeal before they approach others.

Why Are Many Board Members Reluctant to Give (or Even to Discuss Giving)?

Board governance has long been associated with the three Ws, the two Ts, the three Cs, and the way too familiar three Gs. We would like to offer something more positive. But just to review, in case you're not familiar with all the alphabet soup:

The Three Ws
◆ Work
◆ Wealth
◆ Wisdom

The Three Ts
◆ Time
◆ Talent
◆ Treasure

The Three Cs
◆ Cash
◆ Clout
◆ Contacts

And, the dreaded Three Gs

- ◆ Give,
- ◆ Get, or
- ◆ Get off the board

The problem all these philosophies create for nonprofits: do you look for someone who has (and is willing to give you) all three, or do you look for one of these traits in each prospective board member? Ideally, of course, board members would contribute their work, wealth, *and* wisdom; would happily give you their time, talent, *and* treasure; would be able to supply cash, clout, *and* be willing to open the doors to their contacts; and would both give *and* get, so you don't have to ask them to get off. We would like to offer a new way to think about the three Gs.

Our *New* Three Gs

- ◆ Gather
- ◆ Get ready
- ◆ Grow

Try looking at this new way of recruiting and retaining enthusiastic, knowledgeable, and active board members who will embrace their role as a board member, even fundraising!

The First G—Gather

Gather your board together to determine what the board needs in the way of skills, talents, and diversity, and how these attributes can help the organization.

Often bringing in an outside person to do this assessment is useful. Either a paid consultant or perhaps a volunteer from another nonprofit (one with a dynamic, effective board) can help objectively assess your board's performance.

Have the board do a self-assessment of its performance as a whole and as individuals, as we discussed in **Chapter Two**. Perform this assessment on an annual basis. One way to do this is to compile a survey for board members to complete quickly and anonymously. A consultant can design the survey, collect the results, and provide you with a report. You will probably be surprised at the results. We have found that board members often feel they could and should be doing more.

The Second G—Get Ready

Once the board has assessed its makeup and performance, it will need to develop a plan for filling any gaps. Your governance committee, which we'll talk more about, must be in place year-round to coordinate all the activities involved in board development. The best board member you have should chair this committee. After all, this committee holds the future of the board in its hands.

Educate the entire board on the roles and responsibilities of board members and the importance of the board recruitment process. It is in the recruitment process that good boards are created; otherwise, terrible boards result! Before recruiting new board members, assess the current board's strengths and weaknesses, and determine what gaps need to be filled. If you find you need more demographic diversity or more diverse skills and talents, for example, you will know what to look for in new board members.

The Third G—Grow

Once a board profile is complete, a list of potential board members who fill the needs required by the board must be developed. Every board member must understand that just one person on the board never accomplishes board recruitment and that all names must be submitted for approval to the full board before anyone is invited to join the board.

It is also essential that the board position description outlining the roles and responsibilities of individual board members is reviewed with each candidate before being invited to serve on the board. This will be discussed in more detail in the following chapters.

Provide an exciting, compelling board orientation for new board members as well as an ongoing education program for all board members.

The Most Important Qualification of a Board Member

All board and committee members *must* have a passion for the mission of the organization. If they have that passion, it will be easy for them to help in fundraising. They will be eager to do it!

Wrapping It Up

◆ Board giving is critical. Remember, an asker must a giver be!
◆ Many board members don't understand fundraising and will need some education and training.
◆ There are many ways board members can help with fundraising. It's more than asking their friends for money.
◆ Get rid of the old Three Gs mentality and try our *new* Three Gs— gather, get ready, and grow!

Chapter Four

What Do You Need to Look for in Board Members?

I n **Chapter Two,** we discussed the qualities board members should have. Hopefully, you've now been able to evaluate your current board members in these areas and are currently working on a plan to find more good board members with these qualities. Just to refresh you on those qualities, they were:

◆ Are they able to listen, analyze, think clearly and creatively, and work well with people individually and in a group?

◆ Are they willing to prepare for and attend board and committee meetings, ask questions, take responsibility for and follow through on a given assignment, generously contribute personal and financial resources, open doors in the community, and evaluate themselves?

◆ Are they willing to develop skills they do not already possess, such as to cultivate and solicit funds, cultivate and recruit board members and other volunteers, read and understand financial statements, and learn more about the substantive program area of the organization?

◆ Do they possess honesty; sensitivity to and tolerance of differing views; a friendly, responsive, and patient approach; community-building skills; personal integrity; a developed sense of values; concern for your nonprofit's development; and a sense of humor?

Let's elaborate on these qualities and discuss how you determine if prospective board members are right for your organization.

Do They "Play Well with Others?"

Okay, we admit that sometimes people seem like good board material until they're on the board, and you find they are "loose cannons." You should spend enough time with prospective board members, interviewing them just as you would a staff applicant. Often these conversations will reveal that they have had issues in the past serving on other boards and will send up red flags. Pay attention to their statements and questions. If they've complained about other boards they've been on, don't be afraid to talk to other board members and executive directors about how this candidate worked out as a board member for them. Sometimes there are personality clashes, and maybe this person just found themselves in a contentious situation. But, if you talk to three or more other agencies and they've all had issues with this person, it is most likely the individual, and not all the other organizations, that have the problem.

Time Commitment

In the interview process, set clear expectations for the board member's time commitment to the role. Discuss how much time will be spent on board meetings, committee work, attendance at events and activities, fundraising, and other commitments that take their time. If the candidate doesn't have the time to be an active board member, don't accept them just because you need to fill a seat on the board with a warm body. Make it clear that if they don't have the time, but do want to serve your organization, perhaps other roles might interest them. For example, they could serve on a committee or task force or volunteer in some other way. Maybe you have an advisory council that could benefit from their expertise. Do not make exceptions just because you need to fill a seat.

Experience teaches that it's better to have a smaller, active board than a large board that doesn't have a quorum at meetings, and which doesn't participate in committee work, activities, events, and fundraising.

Skills

Another thing you will want to look for in prospective board members is whether they have skills and talents that complement the needs of your organization. Part of the "get ready" phase of our new Three Gs is determining what the needs of your board are. Does your organization need marketing skills, someone with a good handle on technology, an attorney, someone with financial expertise, a board member with experience in fundraising, a person with knowledge of your program, or someone with government contacts? The list will be different for each organization, but it's crucial to develop a list of the skills and talents you need before you start recruiting board members.

One word of caution—sometimes, you find what appears to be a square peg that fits better in a round hole!

For example, before going into the development profession, Linda spent eleven years in banking. During this time, she sat on numerous nonprofit boards. Guess why these nonprofits wanted her. For her financial expertise, of course. And she was always asked to serve on the finance committee of every board she sat on. However, if those nonprofits had been more diligent in the recruitment process, they would have found out that Linda worked in the Private Banking Group and then in the marketing department at the bank. Hence, she was a much better fit for a major gifts committee or a marketing committee. Likewise, she had a friend who was an architect and was always asked to serve on the facilities committee until Linda found herself in a development position at a museum and proposed her friend for a board position. He was happily placed, due to Linda's knowledge of his interest in art, on the collections management committee. So be sure to have meaningful conversations with prospective board members about their skills, talents, and interests. You might be surprised to find some hidden talents that your organization can use!

Integrity

Above all, you want someone who has a passion for your mission and has impeccable integrity. They will take things like transparency and ethical standards seriously. They will reveal conflicts of interest and be careful not to let any of those conflicts cloud their judgment when it comes to making decisions that are in the best interest of your organization. They will be diligent in reviewing IRS Form 990s and audit reports.

Wrapping It Up

◆ Don't skip the "get ready" phase of your board recruitment plan—assess what your needs are and then look for board members who meet those needs.

◆ Make sure prospective board members are aware of the roles, responsibilities, and time commitments of board members before agreeing to serve on the board.

◆ A small, active board is better than a larger, inactive, unaware, ineffective board.

◆ Don't forget to hold meaningful conversations with potential board members before inviting them to serve on the board.

◆ Interview prospective board members with *at least* the thoroughness and thoughtfulness with which you would interview applicants for a staff position.

◆ If a potential board member does not meet your requirements, see if there is another role to offer in your organization. Don't recruit someone just to fill an empty chair at the board table.

◆ Above all, make sure your board members have a passion for your mission and impeccable integrity.

Chapter Five

Creating Position Descriptions

Never, never, never recruit board members unless you have a good position description for the board. Who develops this position description? The board's governance committee should take the primary responsibility for developing this position description, with input from staff and board members. You may want to bring in a governance consultant to help. We are providing you a sample position description below. You can also find sample descriptions from AFP, on the Internet, or from colleagues.

Sample Board Position Description

Board Trustee Job Description

Purpose:

To act as a voting member of the board with full authority and responsibility to develop policies for the operation of the organization; to monitor the organization's financial health, programs, and overall performance; and to provide the chief executive officer with the resources to meet the needs of those persons the organization serves.

The Full Board's Responsibilities:

- Establish policy

- Hire and evaluate the executive director

- Secure adequate funding for the organization

- Monitor finances

- Create and update a long-range plan for the organization

- Select and support the organization's board officers

- Adopt key operating policies; approve contracts as appropriate

Individual Board Member's Duties:

- Attend board meetings regularly

- Become knowledgeable about the organization

- Come to board meetings well prepared and well informed about issues on the agenda

- Contribute to meetings by expressing your point of view

- Consider other points of view, make constructive suggestions, and help the board make decisions that benefit those persons the organization serves

- Serve on at least one committee

- Represent the organization to individuals, the public, and other organizations in a positive and professional manner

- Support the organization through attendance at special events and activities and through meaningful financial contributions; commit to making the organization one of your top two or three charitable priorities

- Assume board leadership roles when asked

- Keep the executive director informed about any concerns the community may have

- Maintain confidentiality of board discussions

Rationale:

Board members set corporate policies and goals and delegate authority to the executive director to implement them in the daytoday management of the organization. Individual members of the board, however, have no authority to act independently of the full board. When they do, it can seriously damage the organization's ability to carry out its mission, board team spirit, and the organization's image in the community. Board members who abuse their position this way need to be talked to, disciplined, or censured.

Board members are also "trustees" of their organization who approve an annual budget that ensures the budget can meet the nonprofit's financial needs. Also, board members monitor the overall financial health of their organization by engaging an auditor and reviewing annual reports of the auditor. The executive director retains responsibility for the day-to-day operational expenditures.

Individual board members should attend all board meetings and actively participate in them and serve on committees or as board officers. Finally, board members have the responsibility to know and fulfill their proper role as board members and to act in the best interest of those persons the organization serves.

Developing Your Position Descriptions

You will also want to develop position descriptions for board officers, committee chairs, and committee members. Everyone who serves on a leadership role must understand their duties and their role in the organizational structure. You should also develop an organizational chart for your board, like the one we gave you in **Chapter Two.**

Position descriptions should be reviewed periodically, and especially when you are restructuring your board. Another critical piece is having a board commitment form that each board member signs on an annual basis, along with their conflict of interest form, which is required by the IRS and reported on the IRS Form 990 annually. A sample commitment form is provided below. You can receive sample conflict-of-interest statements from AFP or BoardSource.

Board of Directors Commitment Form

Effective governance of a community service organization requires a considerable commitment of time and effort on the part of each board member. Members of the ABC board are expected to meet the following expectations:

1. A basic understanding of ABC and its activities.

2. A commitment to the mission and values of ABC

3. Representation of ABC in a manner consistent with board decisions.

4. A time commitment of about 88 hours per year, or an average of seven hours per month on the following activities:

Board meetings:	2 hrs. /mo x 10 mo	= 20
Committee meetings:	3 hrs. /mo x 10 mo	= 30
Other meetings:	2 hrs. /mo x 10 mo	= 20
Orientation & training:	(1 full day /yr.)	= 10
Social activities:	2 to 3 events /yr.	= 8
	Total	88

5. Willingness to attend additional meetings as needed. Preparation for and participation in fundraising: extra time may be required.

6. Regular attendance at board meetings. Preparation, timely arrival, and participation for the entire duration of sessions.

Due to quorum and workload requirements as well as to achieve our goals of sharing and consensus decision-making, consistent attendance is necessary.

Resigning when you become aware of your inability to keep your commitment, and reapplying when you are once again able to meet your commitment, is recommended. If a director misses more than 25 percent of regularly scheduled board meetings, the person's resignation will be formally considered before the next annual general meeting.

7. Membership and participation on at least one committee. Preparation, timely arrival, and participation for the entire duration of meetings. If a director misses more than 25 percent of regularly scheduled committee meetings, the chair of that committee will speak to the person about the absences. If not resolved at the committee level, the chair brings the situation to the board's attention.

8. Responsibility to notify others of one's inability to attend any meeting as far in advance as possible. The chair of the board or appropriate committee should be contacted directly, or a message left for them at ABC office.

9. Responsibility for following up on missed meetings (board, committee) with the chair of the board or appropriate committees as soon as possible.

10. Willingness to act as a mentor for new board members.

11. Participation in the board orientation and training programs.

- In the first year to take part in the complete orientation and training program.

- As an experienced board member, to assist in the delivery of the orientation and training program.

- To take part in the getacquainted portion of the orientation and training program.

Understood and agreed to

Name_____Date_____

Wrapping It Up

◆ You need position descriptions for board members, officers, committee chairs, and committee members.

◆ These position descriptions must be reviewed at the time of the recruitment discussion, not *after* the person as agreed to serve on the board.

◆ The governance committee develops the position descriptions with input from staff and board members.

◆ Once someone has agreed to serve on the board, they should be asked to sign a commitment form and a conflict-of-interest form on an annual basis.

Chapter Six

Where Do You Find Good Board Members?

For most nonprofit organizations, building an effective board is one of the greatest challenges. Where do you find good board members? How do you get them to join the board and become active in fundraising? And how do you keep them involved once they are on the board?

Often good board members are hard to find, and sometimes it is difficult to assess their commitment to the organization until they are already on the boardwhen it is too late! Some boards flounder because there is no clear direction for them, and they haven't bought into the vision of the organization. Finding committed, dedicated board leadership is often a challenge.

Board members are often reluctant to fundraise because they have not been recruited with that purpose in mind. Even if you originally intended for your board to be involved in fundraising, many times board recruiters are reluctant to use the "F" word for fear of scaring off potential members. Many well-intentioned organizations operate under the noble idea that "once they get on our board and see the great work we are doing, they will want to go out and ask for money." Wrong! If board members have not been told upfront that fundraising is a part of their role, they are far less likely to embrace it later when you decide to "slip it into" their job description.

Getting Businesspeople to Serve on Your Board

Many nonprofits have difficulty attracting business leaders to serve on their boards. When they are successful, they often lose those leaders within the first year. Ever wonder why?

Sometimes people who have spent their entire career in nonprofits just cannot relate to their counterparts from the business world. Yes, the nonprofit world is different! Yes, your nonprofit is unique! And yes, you are doing wonderful work that benefits your community. But often, the business leaders you want to involve on your board are looking more for the bottom-line return on investment (ROI) than the smile on a client's face or the fact that a program that's been losing money for years is mission-critical. They will be interested in bringing what works for them to your nonprofit. And they will think in terms of value propositions, market positioning, and brand awareness. Don't know what those are? Ask your business prospects what's vital to achieving success and research their answers. Then ask them to help you make a meaningful difference in those areas.

If you want these individuals to serve, you must know what will make them comfortable and interested, as well as what will make them run for the door. Here's what people tell us about their frustrations with serving on nonprofit boards.

◆ "I got frustrated with 'nonprofit-speak' and meetings that wasted my time."
◆ "I was pigeonholed."
◆ "My talents were not being used."

Nonprofit-speak Versus Business-speak

One businessperson recalled serving on one board where every board meeting was chock-full of acronyms that were meaningless to businesspeople and, to top it off, the meetings started at 7 p.m. and lasted three to four hours. These endless hours were spent listening to reports that could have been sent in advance of the meeting. "After a long workday, I grew pretty weary of that board."

As we said in **Chapter Four**, sometimes a square peg does fit into a round hole! When recruiting new board members, it is critical to meet with each prospective board member and find out what each of them is *really* looking for in serving on your board. Don't automatically assume that just because the person is a CPA, the finance committee is the obvious place to put this new board member.

As we mentioned, Linda spent eleven years in the banking profession, and every time she was asked to serve on a board, she was placed on the finance committee. Guess what, though? She worked in the marketing department of the bank and was not really a "numbers person," even though *one* of her majors in college was banking and finance. Even if you do have a "finance person" as a prospective board member, a person who crunches numbers all day might just be looking for a creative outlet in board service or at least something that isn't part of the person's day-to-day work.

More Board Members Resign for Lack of *Meaningful* Work than from Being *Over-worked!*

Lots of times we are afraid to ask our board members to do too much because we're afraid they will be scared off. We have long felt that what really turns them off is a lack of *meaningful* work.

Another businessperson told us, "I served on one board that didn't have strong committees; all the 'real work' seemed to be handled by the executive committee, of which I was not a part. Meetings did not have any meat to them, decisions had already been made, and there just didn't seem to be anything critical for discussion. I frankly got bored and quickly moved on to another board where I felt *all* the board members were essential to the organization's success. There was meaningful discussion at board meetings about the vision and future of the organization. Also, committee work was challenging but fun!"

Lesson learned: make sure all board members are engaged, see the big picture, and have specific responsibilities that fit into the big picture for which they'll be held accountable.

Finding Prospective Board Members

A lot of organizations struggle because this is how they approach finding new board members:

For most organizations, the nominating committee has two primary functions: to fill vacant board seats and to elect officers of the board. In most cases, this committee is an ad hoc committee appointed by the president or chair a few months before terms are due to expire. Sometimes there isn't even a nominating committee in place. One of the worst examples we've seen about how *not* to recruit board members was at a December board meeting where the executive director announced, "A few of you have terms expiring this month, so we need a few more board members. Anyone have any ideas?" "What's wrong with this picture," we asked ourselves? Several things:

◆ It was December.

◆ The executive director raised the subject.

◆ No one had any ideas (of course, that may have been the good news!)

Even when an organization has a nominating committee to handle this job, it is usually done wrong. Often, by the time the board chair appoints a nominating committee, most of the board members are busy with other committees, and the nominating task seems to fall to someone who has not been tremendously involved in other board work. As a result, those selected for the nominating committee may not be the best and brightest of the board members. The attitude is sometimes, "Well, how much harm can they do on a nominating committee?" The answer is, "A lot!"

We'll talk more about how to fix this in the next chapter, but finding prospective board members is not something you can do by "flying by the seat of your pants."

So, where can you find board members? Some ideas we've seen work include:

◆ If you're seeking more businesspeople for your board, join and get active in your local chamber(s) of commerce. You'll meet lots of businesspeople there if you make an effort to get to know them. Volunteer to serve on a chamber committee where you get to work with these people, see them in action, and learn more about their skills, talents, and interests.

◆ Do a brainstorming session with your board once you've identified the skills and talents needed. Turn these names over to your governance committee for consideration.

◆ Ask your staff—they know people too! Honest, they do!

◆ Look at the non-board members serving on your committees or as volunteers. They are already committed to your organization, you've had a chance to get to know them, and you've seen them in action—good or bad. The good ones might be potential board members.

Wrapping It Up

◆ Don't wait until the end of the year to start searching for good board members. Keep a year-round list of prospective board members.

◆ Know what board members are looking for and what frustrates them.

◆ If you need businesspeople on your board, hang out in places where you'll find them—your local chamber(s) of commerce are the best place to start.

◆ Brainstorm with your board and staff once you know the skills and talents you are looking for.

◆ Committee members and volunteers are the best sources for finding prospective board members.

Chapter Seven

Whose Job Is It to Recruit Board Members?

You may need to rethink *who* does the recruiting of your board members. Instead of a nominating committee that meets once a year to fill vacant seats, you should appoint a year-round governance committee. This committee can also be called the board resources committee or the committee on directorship or any name with which you feel comfortable. Whatever the title, the following are the key functions to remember about this committee:

- ◆ It should meet year-round.
- ◆ It needs to be chaired by one of the strongest persons on the board.
- ◆ Its duties include assessing board performance, both the board as a whole and individual board members.
- ◆ It is responsible for developing or refining board position descriptions.
- ◆ It evaluates the needs of the board and develops a profile of the kinds of people that are needed to fill vacancies on the board.
- ◆ It works with the full board to help find the right people to fill board positions
- ◆ It assures diversity on the board.
- ◆ It implements, along with senior staff members of the organization, board orientation.
- ◆ It is responsible for the ongoing education of the board.

Duties of the Committee

The governance committee, board resource committee, or committee on directorship is perhaps the most important committee of the board, *not an afterthought.* This committee, once in place and before recruiting new board members, should complete a grid analyzing current strengths and weaknesses of the board. Board members should be listed according to the years their terms expire and diversity indicators—ethnicity, gender, geographic location, etc. Skills, talents, and areas of particular expertise should also be listed, along with giving ability and contacts with various groups such as media, funders, and government agencies. Once this grid is complete, the committee can determine where the gaps are in board diversity, skills, and abilities. A profile can then be developed for the recruitment of new board members.

The committee then takes the results of the assessment to the full board and asks for names to be considered for nomination to the board. Individual board members should *never* haphazardly, or on their own, recruit new board members. Names and resumes are given to the board resource committee, governance committee, or committee on directorship for *consideration.* No one should ever be approached with an automatic assumption that they will be invited to serve on the board, but rather that the committee is considering their name.

The committee then arranges a meeting with the prospective board member. The executive director should be included in this meeting. Board position descriptions are shared with the potential board members and expectations of both the organization and the prospective board member discussed. Once the committee members have a slate of candidates to present, names are then brought to the full board for approval. Once the board elects the new candidates, the committee invites them to join the board and attend their first board meeting.

The committee is also responsible for providing orientation for new board members and may implement a "Board Buddy," or mentoring program, for new board members. This committee also makes recommendations for board officers to be presented to the full board for election. And, the same thought process that goes into recruiting new board members should go into the board officer selection. A succession plan and cultivation of strong board leadership is essential. Board members will follow the example of the board leadership. A strong board chair results in a strong board.

Ongoing board education is also a responsibility of this committee and can significantly improve the effectiveness of the board. As an example, this committee might arrange for caseworkers to make presentations at a board meeting of a human service agency. Or the curator of fine arts might provide education for museum board members. The committee should evaluate the needs for board education and work with the executive director to provide the appropriate educational segments at board meetings or retreats.

One of the critical roles of this important committee is to develop a board position description that includes a required financial contribution from each board member. It also articulates the expectation that each board member be involved in the organization's fundraising efforts through attendance at events, planning development activities, and helping to identify, cultivate, and solicit potential donors.

This committee is also responsible for assuring that the position descriptions are not glossed over during the recruitment process and to make sure that each prospective board member understands that fundraising is an integral part of his or her role as a board member. Committee members must deal with potential board members who are reluctant to accept their fundraising responsibility. It is better to turn away a prospective board member who is not willing to get involved in fundraising than to fill a seat with a warm body just so the committee can say it has met its expectation to bring on a certain number of new board members each year. Instead, invite the reluctant potential board member to serve on a committee or in some other volunteer position where the fit it better than serving as on the board.

The goal is to create a standing governance committee that works thoughtfully and diligently. If you can achieve it, it can make all the difference between a productive, enthused, and inspired board and a lackadaisical board that does not understand its role in advancing the organization's mission and is reluctant to get involved in the fundraising process. It is crucial that this committee, meeting on a year-round basis, evaluate any problems that may arise with the board as a whole or with individual board members.

Wrapping It Up

◆ The governance committee is the most critical committee on your board. In its hands lies the future of your board.

◆ This committee has a year-round job; it should not be an ad hoc committee appointed late in the year.

◆ No one other than the governance committee should try to recruit board members.

◆ The committee should seek input from the board and staff.

◆ This committee also has the responsibility for board orientation and education.

Chapter Eight

What is the Process for Recruiting Board Members?

As we discussed, the governance committee is responsible for ensuring that the position descriptions are not glossed over during the recruitment process and for making sure that each potential board member understands the roles and responsibilities of board service. Expect members of this committee to deal with potential board members who are reluctant to accept their responsibilities. Instead, invite a reluctant prospective board member to serve on a committee or in some other volunteer position rather than on the board.

So, all this is designed to help you recruit the right board members.

Often, boards are reluctant to fundraise because they have not been recruited with that purpose in mind. For many organizations, fundraising has never been a part of their culture for various reasons—perhaps, in the past, they relied on government funding, fees for service, or foundation grants. Then suddenly, when these funding sources shift priorities and income streams dry up, the organization decides it now needs to rethink fundraising and is stymied by how to introduce this concept to the board.

Even if the organization intended initially for its board to be involved in fundraising, many times, board recruiters are reluctant to use the "F" word for fear of scaring off potential board members. Many well-intentioned boards operate under the noble idea that "once they get on our board and see the great work we are doing, they will want to go out and ask for money." Wrong! If they have not been told upfront that fundraising is a part of their role, they will likely not embrace it later when you decide to slip it into their job description.

Who Sits In On the Meetings with Prospective Board Members?

Generally, one member of the governance committee, the executive director, and the person who knows this prospect best, should be in on the initial meeting. Sometimes candidates will want to know more about the organization so that subsequent sessions may be needed. If they have specific questions about programs, development, finance, etc. a staff member or board member specializing in that area may be brought into the next meeting.

Be sure to be open and honest with prospective board members. Be prepared to answer questions they might have. Some questions that potential board members might (and should) ask of you, or of themselves, include:

◆ What are the organization's mission, vision, and values?

◆ Am I passionate about the organization's mission and purpose?

◆ What is the organization's history? Major accomplishments?

◆ Is there a board position description?

◆ What do I bring to the organization? (How will my talents be used?)

◆ How often does the board meet, and when? How long are the meetings?

◆ May I see a current board roster?

◆ How many board members regularly attend meetings? Is there usually a quorum?

◆ Are board meeting agendas and information sent in advance?

◆ What is the financial expectation for board members?

◆ Does the organization have directors and officers (D & O) liability insurance?

◆ Does the organization have a strategic plan?

◆ How often is the strategic plan updated?

◆ How does the organization orient new board members?

◆ How is the board organized? Are committee recommendations respected?

◆ Is the organization's IRS Form 990 current? Does the board review it before it's filed?

◆ Does the board review monthly/regular financial statements? May I review a copy?

◆ Do board meeting minutes reflect the board's decision-making process?

◆ Are board meeting minutes reviewed and approved regularly?

◆ Does the board hold an annual self-evaluation and apply best practices?

◆ How does the board handle a conflict of interest? Is there a conflict-of-interest form to be signed?

◆ What are the terms for board members and elected officers?

◆ Are the organization's bylaws current? May I review a copy?

◆ Is there a board policy manual?

◆ Are there any pending legal issues facing the organization?

People considering board membership have a right to ask these questions and receive forthright answers. You should prepare a board recruitment packet including things like your annual report, strategic plan, bylaws, most recent IRS Form 990, board organizational chart, list of current board members, and board job description.

Don't forget that you also have a right to ask prospective board members questions, such as:

◆ What are they hoping to get out of this experience?

◆ What previous board experience have they had—good or bad?

◆ Are they willing to make the commitments as described in the position description?

◆ Do they have any real or perceived conflicts of interest?

◆ Are they able to attend board meetings regularly?

◆ On what committees would they like to serve?

◆ Do they understand the financial commitment expected?

◆ Are they willing to get involved in fundraising?

◆ Do they know the roles and responsibilities of the board?

Once the governance committee and people interviewing the candidate are comfortable that there is a good fit, the candidate's name is then presented to the full board for consideration and possible confirmation. This will usually take at least two interviews with serious candidates. And there you go, it's as simple as that! Well, maybe not *simple,* but trust us, a thoughtful recruitment process will save you time, money, and aggravation in the long run.

Wrapping It Up

◆ There should be a team interviewing prospective board members.

◆ Remember, a good board member will ask all the right questions; be prepared to answer them.

◆ You also have the right to ask questions and get honest answers.

◆ Only after you're sure the prospective board member is a good fit does the name get presented to the full board for consideration.

Chapter Nine

Retaining Good Board Members

So, we've talked about evaluating your board as well as finding prospective five-star board members, who should recruit them, and how to recruit them. Now that you've got them, how do you keep them?

Keeping Your Board Enthused

Once you've built the board you want, how do you keep the board members enthused and active? A few hints:

- ◆ Have enough committee members to share the workload.
- ◆ Make sure board and committee meetings are productive.
- ◆ Ensure that meetings start and end on time.
- ◆ Send agendas and committee reports in advance of meetings.
- ◆ Have term limits and enforce them to avoid perpetual board members and avoid founder's syndrome.
- ◆ Provide education and training for the board in areas where they need to be knowledgeable.

The Dreaded Board "Training"

Building a capable and enthusiastic board is one of the most critical elements in successful nonprofits. But, of course, your board members don't think they need training, they don't have time for it, and they won't listen to what you say anyway.

Try calling board training by a more meaningful title, perhaps Executive Leadership Symposium!

You can get your board members excited about fundraising by selecting the one individual on your board who most "gets it" about fundraising and have this individual chair your development committee. This board member's enthusiasm will be contagious and may even spur fundraising competition among board members. You can also try bringing in a consultant to help motivate the board. If your organization cannot afford a consultant, try inviting a board member from a nonprofit whose board has been successful at fundraising to talk to your board about its role in fundraising. Be sure to select this person carefully. You don't want someone who will just brag about the fundraising success of the other nonprofit's board, try to shame your board members into fundraising, or get dragged into the morass of a stagnant board. You want someone who will inspire and motivate your board.

Make sure your board members understand the importance of having a development plan that covers all areas of fundraising, from events to major gifts and planned gifts. Your development committee should be deeply involved in formulating this plan and presenting it to your board. It is better to have your board members ask other board members to get involved in fundraising than for staff to be the ones who insist on board involvement.

If your organization is overly involved in special events, board members can easily get burned out. Your board members will not be happy if they are expected to sell tickets to their friends and family members for too many special events. Many of them will not be interested in golf, running, dancing, or whatever these events involve. You need to focus on one or two successful events and stress the board's attendance to show the community that the board supports your organization. You will be more successful in enlisting their participation if you involve board members in planning these events.

Board education is essential. The timing of this education, however, is a critical element. You should prepare some type of board education at every board meeting—even if it's a ten-minute presentation on the role of boards in nonprofits, ethical issues for boards, making a case for your organization. You get the idea. For more intense sessions, schedule a time convenient for most board members. Often a Saturday morning or a two-hour session in place of—or before or after—a regular board meeting works well. Once a year, take your board away from the organization for a day-long retreat that includes some educational opportunities as well as time to plan.

Staff can lead board educational sessions, but they're usually more effective when brought from an outside perspective. Education needs to be ongoing but should be done in "chunks" of time and information given. Board members who have never raised funds can't grasp it all in one sitting.

A consultant, a board member from another organization, a video from BoardSource, or some other resource can often tell your board the things they need to hear in a new light.

One of the most important things you can do for your board is to provide a "mission moment" at each board meeting to remind board members why you exist and why their work is vital to your community. It helps board members focus on the importance of your mission before they get into discussions of budget, facilities, program, and personnel, and inspires them to get involved in fundraising.

Wrapping It Up

◆ Plan a proper board orientation, so board members get off on the right foot.

◆ Plan your board meetings, so they are a good use of board members' time.

◆ Recruit non-board members for some of your board committees.

◆ Provide ongoing education in specialty areas.

◆ Plan a "mission moment" at every board meeting.

◆ Make board expectations clear from the very beginning

◆ Don't be afraid to fire or reassign board members.

Chapter Ten

Bringing it All Together

We've tried to summarize our combined years of experience as development directors, executive director, and board members so you can have that five-star board about which we all dream. But it doesn't have to be a dream if you follow the steps in this book.

To sum it up:

- ◆ Start by getting rid of your nominating committee and replacing it with a year-round governance committee.
- ◆ Review job descriptions, board commitment forms, board profile forms, and conflict-of-interest statements.
- ◆ Review your bylaws and make changes where needed to term limits, committee structure, etc.
- ◆ Engage a governance consultant, if needed.
- ◆ Analyze board demographics, skills, talents, interests.
- ◆ Have your current board members do a self-evaluation of their involvement with your organization.
- ◆ Decide if you need to fire some board members, re-engage them, or move them into some other role.
- ◆ Develop an ideal board-member profile.
- ◆ Develop a list of prospective board members that fit this profile.
- ◆ Conduct interviews with potential board members and recommend the ones most suitable for your board.
- ◆ Develop a board orientation and ongoing education program.

Feel free to contact us if you have questions about anything covered in this book. We have a lot of success stories you might learn from—and some horror stories which might help you avoid some of the mistakes we've seen.

And don't forget about our ongoing courses, webinars, and books that can help you.

We wish you success in building your five-star board!

Additional Resources

Books:

◆ *You and Your Nonprofit Board*
https://lindalysakowskicourses.com/books-by-linda/you-and-your-nonprofit-board

◆ *CharityChannel's Quick Guide to Board Giving*
https://lindalysakowskicourses.com/books-by-linda/charitychannels-quick-guide-to-board-giving

Courses:

◆ Be the Best Board Member You Can Be
https://lindalysakowskicourses.com/courses-by-linda/be-the-best-board-member-you-can-be/

◆ Build a Great Board
https://lindalysakowskicourses.com/courses-by-linda/build-a-great-board/

www.ingramcontent.com/pod-product-compliance
Lightning Source LLC
Chambersburg PA
CBHW071521210326
41597CB00018B/2831